I KILLED
A RABID FOX
WITH A
CROQUET MALLET

MAKING YOUR BUSINESS STORIES
COMPELLING AND MEMORABLE

HB Books * HB Agency * Boston

HB Books   *   HB Agency   *   Boston

HB Books
Hart-Boillot, LLC
134 Rumford Avenue
Newton, Massachusetts 02466
www.hbagency.com

ISBN: 978-0-9892355-0-1

First Edition 2013

Designed by Justin Hastings, Christine Tesseo, and Kevin Hart

Printed in the United States of America

TABLE OF CONTENTS

FOREWARD

Over the last two decades, I have read innumerable books on story telling, each offering its own version of the importance of story in human interaction. Many of these books presented compelling and memorable stories, tales that stick in my mind long after I've read them. I've come across comments, quotes and books on storytelling by great writers from Ernest Hemingway to Anton Chekhov, Hollywood producers and directors from George Lucas to Michael Curtis, and even the greats of advertising, such as David Ogilvy.

The advice they offer is often difficult, if not impossible, to put into action. Many of the story-writing books offer examples – often hundreds of pages worth – that keep us reading because of who they feature, not what they teach. Obviously, we want to read examples of how Nelson Mandela, Pat Riley, Oprah, Ellen DeGeneres, Jack Welch or Bill Clinton used stories to move people and achieve success. We buy those books and read their stories because we already know something about these people. Whether we admire them or not, we like to learn more about their lives, dig into the details that fascinate us and discover more reasons to love them or hate them – either way, we continue reading.

But there's a big difference between watching an expert and being an expert. You're not likely to watch Tiger Woods swing a club and be able to do it just like him moments later. Most of us need instruction that breaks down the swing into each of its constituent parts, in such a way that we can create our own best game. We need an instructor who does more than simply show us how it's done – an instructor who understands that watching the PGA Tour will not give us all we need to know. This instructor must speak to us in our own language – the language of one who hasn't reached perfection – so that we can relate, understand, and learn.

That's not to say it's amateur hour here at Story Central. On the contrary, the beauty of learning to craft and tell great stories is that you can improve this skill each day until the end of your life. With improvement will come more and more of what you want, whether it's simply to become a more effective communicator or to tell stories to gain recognition and increase financial success.

In this book, we took a lesson from a small volume that has done wonders for our business: *The E-Myth*. In that book, Michael Gerber focuses on a single example, a small pie-making business, to help entrepreneurs understand the difference between creating a job and building a business. He does not use multinational corporations as examples or rely on world-famous celebrities to make his arguments. He must have understood that such examples might sell books but do not offer the lessons most of us need to grow our businesses.

I Killed a Rabid Fox with a Croquet Mallet does the same – while we might refer to some of the world's great companies once in a while, our examples come from businesses we can easily understand, many of which we have worked with as a marketing agency. These businesses look and feel like many small and medium-sized businesses worldwide. From a small Canadian folk band, to a medium-sized environmental consulting group, our examples help you to see that it's not such a stretch to get from here to there, using your own best stories as the catalyst. You can do it, and this book will show you how.

ACKNOWLEDGMENTS

The first person to thank is Robert McKee, story-doctor to the world's best film studios, mentor to numerous Oscar-winning screenwriters and Emmy-winning television writers, instructor to communications professionals, scholar, actor, director, author, and leader of the extraordinary McKee Story Seminars, three of which I have attended. His work has inspired much of this book, has helped me drive HB Agency – a marketing firm working in business-to-business and business-to-consumer markets – to create the best possible stories for its clients. It has inspired my appreciation for stories and their lasting power. This year, 2013, Robert McKee will introduce a new Business Story Seminar, which I'm sure will be a "must-attend" for anyone in the communications business and certainly anyone who has picked up this book.

I have been writing this book in one form or another for over five years. In 2011 I decided it was time to get it done, and it has taken me another two years to do that. During that time, I have benefited from contributions from Amanda Griffith (Bumble PR), and numerous colleagues at HB Agency, most notably Kevin Hart, Andrea Dunbeck, Jennifer O'Connell, Mark O'Toole and Justin Hastings. Many others helped along the way – and the whole team at HB Agency gave me great leeway to do the bulk of this writing. I thank them for their patience as I tried to get it right.

Finally, an enormous thank-you to my business partner, Kevin Hart, president and creative director at HB. He not only agreed to the investment in time and money this book has required, but he came up with the title.

Because of the many contributors to the ideas and pages in this book, I'm using the first-person plural, "we," as the narrative voice.

Nicolas Boillot
CEO, HB Agency

CHAPTER 1

WHAT'S A STORY?

Search online or ask friends and colleagues, "What's in a story?" and each friend, each source, will give you a different answer.

In HB Agency's PR practice, when we reach out to journalists, they often ask right away if we're calling about a first, best or only. In other words, they want to know if our scoop will provide them with knowledge about a product, service or even an event that no one has ever heard about. Or something that's more impressive than anything else. If we can't say "yes" (and most of the time we can't), they ask, "Why would my audience care?"

Novelist Jim Hines says he was taught that a story shows us "interesting people in interesting places solving interesting problems in interesting ways." He goes on to ask, "What qualifies as interesting, anyway?" And, "How can you tell if your stuff will be interesting to others?"

Great past and contemporary storytellers will refer to Shakespeare as the master of all storytellers, yet after in-depth study, none of them can devise any sort of recipe for telling a great story based on Shakespeare.

Some Shakespearean scholars claim that he relied on surprise and incongruity for much of his storytelling – that those elements, surprise and incongruity, keep us hooked as his plots unfold. *Surprise and incongruity, what am I supposed to do with that?*

Roughly 400 years after Shakespeare, Robert McKee, consultant to the film industry and mentor to screenwriters, novelists and playwrights, often says "story happens when there's a gap between expectation and result." That's a little more helpful than "surprise and incongruity." In fact, that nugget is so helpful that it bears repeating:

STORY HAPPENS WHEN THERE'S A GAP BETWEEN EXPECTATION AND RESULT.

Let's dig deeper.

Suppose you run into an old friend at a business meeting and you say, "Hey, have I got a story for you!" She perks up, and you start off:

> *"I went to work late yesterday evening to finish up a project, and my business partner was already in his office. I could tell by the light under the door. Wow, I thought, he's not usually in that late. I knocked on the door, he told me to come in, and then he had this situation going on which made me want to help him right away..."*

Very quickly, you notice that your old friend has that sleepy look in her eye that you recognize from somewhere. Oh, that's it: the same look a two-year-old gets when her mother reads *Goodnight Moon*.

Try again:

> *"I went to work late yesterday evening and my business partner was in his office. I knocked on the door, walked in, and noticed that things weren't right. I had had some suspicion about this because he's not usually in his office. He was actually lying on the floor..."*

She perks up. What? Lying on the floor? Try once more:

> *"I went to work late last night and found my business partner lying on the floor naked with scratch marks all over his body. I heard a noise and looked up to see an orangutan in the corner, glaring at me while chewing one of its fingernails..."*

Your colleague interrupts you. "Whoooa..." she says, "slow down. I want to hear it from the beginning... so you're walking into the office and... did you even notice *anything* on your way in?"

You didn't even have to get loud or intense.

The widening gap between expectation and result, and/or the surprise and incongruity that Shakespeare relies on, absorbs us into the story. At this point you might be thinking: *Makes sense. But my company doesn't have stories about naked business partners recently mauled by orangutans!*

NEWS FLASH: YOU HAVE STORIES, MANY OF THEM COMPELLING.

Your stories exist. They're told and repeated every day:
- By directors, to management
- By management, to employees
- By salespeople, to customers
- By customers, to prospects

Some people might not even think of them as stories, but you have them in droves and they survive and propagate, with or without your assistance. Unfortunately, they're most often forgotten, wasted or poorly used.

LEVERAGE - MAKING MORE FROM WHAT YOU'VE GOT.

Remember your first experience of leverage. Maybe you had to move a rock and someone showed you how you could put your weight on one end of a stick, use a log or a boulder as a fulcrum, and move a heavy object on the other end. You didn't have to change your weight or your strength. You didn't have to buy any additional equipment. But suddenly you could leverage your own weight to move something much bigger.

Stories are like that. You've got them and you've already paid for them. They can do the heavy lifting for you and your business. The question is how to make the most of them, to leverage them, in order to move your audiences the way you want.

NEWS FLASH - YOU ABSORB OTHER BUSINESSES' STORIES EVERY DAY.

From billboards to the Internet, businesses compete to inform, interact, transact and create strong relationships with prospects and customers. L.L.Bean rose to fame through its ironclad satisfaction guarantee:

> *"Guaranteed to Last^{SM}. Our products are guaranteed to give*

100% satisfaction in every way. Return anything purchased from us at anytime if it proves otherwise. We do not want you to have anything from L.L.Bean that is not completely satisfactory."

When we were in college, students boasted about returning an item they had abused over several months or years and getting a new one for free. Such stories spread quickly. We believe L.L.Bean banked on the fact that most people who heard these stories had one reaction: *That person's abusing the system. But what an amazing company to have such a return policy!*

The return policy doesn't make the story interesting – it's the story about someone abusing the system that captures our attention. Did L.L.Bean executives plan on such stories becoming the catalyst to its phenomenal growth and longevity? Maybe they knew that some bargain-hunters and system abusers would be the first to spread tales about the return policy. If so, they must also have known that such tales would reach and influence millions of

{ **When you do have a good story, when you know it inside and out, and you tell it well, isn't it an amazing experience?**

shoppers who would be more scrupulous about their returns.

OUTSIDE BUSINESS, WE RECOGNIZE STORIES EVERYWHERE.

Great stories live in movies, theatres, magazine pages, YouTube, books, company websites and, most of all, in our minds.

Great stories stick out and stick around. We retell them. We re-read them. We watch them repeated. We share them over and over again. In fact, we like them so much that we rely on other people to point out, *you've told me that one already.* To which we answer, "I know. But Joe hasn't heard it – I'll tell it again." Sometimes we even say, "I know, but I like telling it."

NO MATTER WHAT THEY SAY, YOU CAN LEARN TO TELL A GOOD STORY.

From the gossip we pick up around the office to the soap operas we watch on TV (and yes, *Mad Men* is a soap opera), we crave good stories and we love to hear them and repeat them as often as we're allowed.

But many of us think, *I don't tell that good a story – let Jane tell it. She does a better job.*

And that thought permeates and poisons all our storytelling, whether at home or at work.

Yet when you do have a good story, when you know it inside and out, and you tell it well, isn't it an amazing experience?

> *But isn't that just luck, or the moment, or my mood, or the audience, or the alcohol?*

No.

THERE'S A METHOD!

Believe it or not, good storytellers have a method to their

madness. Doesn't this make sense? After all, people go to school to learn engineering, medicine, computer science and languages. Some people have aptitudes for all these subjects, just the way some people are natural storytellers, but even those with existing skills can learn to do better with training and practice. Just because someone was good at dissecting in school doesn't mean you want her to perform your surgery before she's gone to medical school!

Even the best natural storytellers benefit from years of practice. Think about that as "on-the-job learning." But most of us have to learn how to tell a good story starting from the basics. Because we weren't natural storytellers, we didn't gravitate to practicing on the job for years. And over time, our confidence suffered.

Don't worry. If you can learn to make a widget or provide a service, you can certainly learn to tell a story. Particularly if that story will help you sell more widgets or services!

NEWS FLASH: YOU DON'T NEED 10,000 HOURS

In his book *Outliers: The Story of Success*, Malcolm Gladwell convincingly argues that it takes 10,000 hours to perfect a skill. But making your business stories better shouldn't require that kind of investment.

Remember Robert McKee, the Hollywood "script doctor" we mentioned earlier? His Story Seminar has been the ultimate class for over 50,000 screenwriters, filmmakers, TV writers, novelists, industry executives, actors, producers, directors, playwrights and advertising professionals. As of this writing, McKee's students have won:

- 35 Academy Awards (160+ nominations)
- 164 Emmy Awards (500+ nominations)
- 29 WGA Awards (77+ nominations)
- 25 DGA Awards (48+ nominations)

We have a feeling there are more than a few Clio Awards in there as well.

Will you be winning awards with your business' stories? Probably not, because that probably would take 10,000 hours, and you have a day job. But that doesn't mean you have to look forward to a life of dull stories and boring marketing content. You can still apply some of McKee's wisdom. For starters:

"...the writer must study the elements of story as if they were instruments of an orchestra – first separately, then in concert."

For the purpose of this book, you are "the writer." Now let's look at the elements of story.

COMPELLING AND MEMORABLE

These terms will crop up repeatedly throughout this book. Most people talk about stories and describe them as good, great, cool, fun, etc. Qualifiers like these are completely subjective. And while almost everything qualifies as "subjective" to some degree, using the words compelling and memorable is more helpful to helping us understand what makes a story valuable for your business.

Compelling: This means that the story grabs your attention. You are compelled to listen, read, and watch. We're not naïve enough to think that many business stories will provide edge-of-your-seat gripping intensity... But compelling, yes. Even captivating. The right business stories grab the audience's attention, just like the right salesperson hooks a prospect.

But who's the "you" when we say *grab your attention*? It's not you! You're the storyteller. While your story should seem compelling to you, it's more important to make it compelling for your audience. Remember that – we'll be talking about audience later.

Memorable: As business owners and employees, we attribute special meaning to some of our stories. They color the fabric of our time together, the ups and downs of our business life, the solidarity of being "in it together." They often provide reasons for getting up each day and going to work – reasons we tell friends and loved ones on a regular basis. This book is about stories designed especially for your professional communities, inside and outside your business, and we want them memorable for two primary reasons.

- First, we need our audiences, especially our customers and prospects, to maintain great reasons to work with us.

In a fiercely competitive landscape, it's tough to get a new customer. Keeping that customer happy is even tougher. What we call brand loyalty involves getting customers to remember compelling stories about our business and their interactions with it. For our internal audiences, the same reasoning applies: Memorable stories solidify an employee's reasons to go back to work, to talk to other potentially good employees about the company, and to value the memories he or she makes in the workplace.

- Second, one of the best ways to market ourselves is when other people market for us – in other words, word of mouth marketing. If our audiences remember the great stories about our business, they will much more easily share them with their friends. In a time when the networked world makes sharing easier than ever, it pays to have plenty of good stories to share.

CHAPTER 2

WHY DO YOU NEED A
GOOD STORY
WHEN YOU HAVE A GOOD BUSINESS?

Can you describe your product or service using the words *first*, *best* or *only*?

If not, what do you really have? What makes you think anyone will consider your company more than a "me-too"?

Let's face it, most businesses are me-toos. Many survive and some thrive. Look around at all the me-toos you use in your business and personal life: cameras, scanners, PCs, dry cleaners, restaurants, office supply stores, cookware, cars, bicycles and clothes. The list is endless.

What you might not realize is that being first, best or only is over-rated. While we all strive for it, the truth is that many of us won't achieve it. We can still do well. And we can look at many first, best or only companies and see that they never approached our success. Did you know the first commercial computer was a UNIVAC, designed by Presper Eckert and John Mauchly? Where are Eckert, Mauchly and UNIVAC now? Some of the first commercial vacuum cleaners were Hoovers. In fact, Hoover did so well that the brand became the de-facto name for vacuuming for many years. But do you use a Hoover?

For me-toos like most of our businesses, and even for many first, best or only companies, the world is filled with products and services that look and sound just like ours. With so much noise, the competition is brutal. You need to distinguish yourself. This is where your stories make the difference.

EACH OF US HAS A STORY. YOU PROBABLY HAVE MANY.

You're likely to tell some of your stories. But unlike your parents, who were eager to hear your stories as you learned to tell them, most people barely listen. Of the stories they listen to, very few, if any, are remembered. And when we say "very few," we're being optimistic. Consider your personal and business acquaintances. Pick three who aren't in your immediate circle of friends and family – quickly. Picture them. Try to remember one or two stories about each of them. If you can, you're unusual – and probably a good listener.

Or you have fascinating acquaintances. But chances are, neither of these is the case.

The point is that good stories are a rare pleasure, and when we hear one, we tell it over and over again. We even tell it to people who don't care. We even tell it when we're not good at storytelling, and we know that people won't enjoy and remember it the way we did. Why? Because it's a good story. Everybody loves a good story.

BUT LET'S FACE IT, THE AVERAGE STORY IS DULL AND FORGETTABLE.

The worst are unendurable. The good news is we're all in the same boat. Not only do our stories sometimes lack substance, but even when they're good, we often don't know how to tell them.

Even the word "story" doesn't mean much anymore. People who toss around that word use it to describe anything from a headline to a tweet. There's even an online tool called Storify. The tool allows you to search for social media content from Twitter, Facebook, YouTube, Flickr, Instagram and more, arrange them, comment and contextualize, and build a story. It's a great idea: People can conduct research in the media they care about most and use that research to create a story. Unfortunately, most people lack an understanding of what makes a story. The Storify site shows examples of real stories being delivered through Storify, such as a moment-by-moment story about a raging wildfire. But it gives little insight into what will make the story compelling or memorable.

A wildfire is interesting by its very nature – our brains are programmed to respond to things like wildfires, if only for self-protection. But not all stories benefit from such a hook.

One "Storify" story, at the time of this writing, is entitled: "The Best Romney Car Elevator Gags – Here are a few of the many Twitter jokes about how the Republican candidate's house is outfitted."

There's nothing wrong with delivering such content to audiences. But it's not a story, and using the "S" word indiscriminately confuses the people who wish to create compelling and memorable stories for their businesses. How can a marketing manager be expected to create great content when he doesn't even know how to define great content? How can CEOs help choose the stories that best showcase their business' capabilities when their employees think that any content can be used to make a story? Some even think that tweeting about a product update is tantamount to producing content that customers will love and remember? And what's the point again?

WHY DOES MY BUSINESS NEED GOOD STORIES?

Jack Welch, longtime Chairman and CEO of GE, credits part of his success to the fact that he's good at telling stories. Why should this matter to you?

- If you want your customers to keep you top-of-mind…
- If you want customers to refer you, and prospects to remember you…
- If you want employees to talk about your organization in memorable ways…
- If you want to make an impression that lasts longer than a conversation…

Then you need good stories.

> *But how do I do it? I don't even think I have good stories, and how do I pick from the ones I do have?*

Hold on to such questions, and add a couple: Which stories are worth telling? How do you make sure your stories reach, touch, move, inspire, humor, or change your audience in some way?

This book answers such questions, and we wrote it because we have seen how great stories can help businesses and organizations. In fact, we've been lucky enough to help our clients craft some of those customer-moving stories. Understanding, building and deploying your business' stories may be the single most important thing you do when it comes to marketing yourself or your organization. With this book's help, you will turn your stories into rocket fuel for your business.

CHAPTER 3

SO WHAT'S IN
A STORY?

You must be wondering, *When do I learn how to tell a good story? Is it only "when a gap opens up between expectation and result?"*

It starts there, but it's a lot more. Read on, and you will begin to change the way you think about stories. Be prepared for a little work, but know that there's good news at the end. Businesses thrive on sharing stories, and good stories can lead to the biggest deals in a business' trajectory.

The Hollywood producer, entrepreneur, music industry leader, writer and UCLA professor Peter Guber, writes: "…stories have a unique power to move people's hearts, minds, feet and wallets in the story teller's intended direction."

That quote comes from the first pages of his book *Tell to Win: Connect, Persuade, and Triumph with the Hidden Power of Story*, in which he chronicles stories from some of the world's great achievers and how those stories played pivotal roles in their triumphs. Guber notes that it's critical to train yourself to tell stories well. And even if you're great at what you do, telling stories about it might not come easy. Is it mandatory? No, but if you don't do it…

IF YOUR BUSINESS DOESN'T TELL COMPELLING AND MEMORABLE STORIES, IT MEANS UNIMAGINABLE AMOUNTS OF LOST REVENUE!

Hard to believe? Think of all the people your business reaches, and imagine if every person touched by your business remembered a great story about it… can you quantify what that would provide in terms of word-of-mouth advertising and repeat business? How would that kind of impression in your audiences' minds impact sales?

When we were in college, we kept hearing about the L.L.Bean return policy we mentioned earlier. Today, over twenty-five years since some of us graduated, that return policy still motivates us to shop at L.L.Bean. An informal poll among people we know who feel the same way reveals that returns have been few and far between.

How many businesses do you support without even thinking about it, without ever considering a competitor? How many times do you think, *I should probably check out other suppliers/vendors/ contractors*, but you don't? We tell ourselves it's too much trouble, but really we're reacting to a visceral bond with that business, a bond that most often has formed over meaningful stories. The more compelling those stories, the less likely we are to switch to a competitor.

STORIES ARE NOT FACTS AND FIGURES!

Don't mistake organizing facts with telling a story. Most businesses are good at organizing their facts. Millions of case studies, product sheets, and menus of services sit and grow moldy with disuse on websites and in brochures and binders... unread and often unremembered. Some businesses even call these product briefs and case studies "stories." But look at them closely, and you'll realize they're just organized facts, or in many cases, disorganized facts.

When businesses bring together their facts, they usually organize them into categories that are similar and repeatable across a range

> **These two basic concepts - story values and events - matter most when telling compelling business stories.**

of different cases or briefs. They fill these standard "buckets of information" with all the facts they can find about each case. Most of the time, the buckets are labeled with words like "Challenge," "How We Approached the Problem," and "Solution." Or "Problem," "Industry Solution," and "Our Solution."

Don't despair – organizing your facts is easy to do and moves your business a huge step in the right direction. But the next step requires a little more thought. Instead of "buckets of information," we're asking you to consider elements of story. If you apply them well and regularly, not only will your stories become more fun to tell, but they'll be more memorable for your listener.

Think of what architects need to know when designing a house. They need to have a way into the house. That might be a swinging door, or a sliding door, or a tunnel... but the house won't work without some way to get inside.

A story is like that. It won't be compelling or memorable without certain key components. This might feel artificial, but consider it training. Even the best cook needs to use a recipe once in a while, and many great cooks started out trying thousands of recipes before "winging it." By the time you finish this book, you'll have your own recipe for how to tell a good story. If you learn it, you'll soon be winging it successfully in all areas of your life, from the boardroom to the banquet room.

STORY VALUES AND EVENTS

These two basic concepts – story values and events – matter most when telling compelling business stories. They also matter most when telling non-business stories, and Robert McKee, mentioned earlier, writes and speaks a great deal about both values and events.

STORY VALUES

In his book *Story: Substance, Structure, Style and the Principles of Screenwriting*, McKee tells us, "Story values are the universal qualities of human experience that may shift from positive to negative, or negative to positive, from one moment to the next."

So what does that mean, in terms of business? Think of what shifts from negative to positive, and vice-versa, for your company and your work life:

- profitable/unprofitable (company, product lines, quarters)
- capable/incapable (employees, products, services, teams, customers)
- optimistic/pessimistic (employees, management, customers)
- favorable/unfavorable (marketplace, weather, rules and regulations, competitive landscape)
- experienced/inexperienced (employees, management, customers, partners)
- reliable/unreliable (employees, customers, competitors)
- innovative/stagnant (industry, company, teams)
- growing/shrinking (budgets, bottom line, market share)
- thriving/failing (company, people)
- hard working/lazy (employees, customers)
- efficient/inefficient (technology, people)
- closed sale/lost sale (needs no explanation!)
- happy/unhappy (customers, employees, management, etc)

These are values, and as you think about your own business, you might come up with many more. In our integrated marketing business, "original/cliché" and "brilliant/unremarkable" are primary value sets we use to rate our ideas. For one of our manufacturing clients, key values include "busy/idle" or "leading edge/archaic," and even "safe/toxic." Obviously, these are not all universal qualities of human experience, but many of them qualify as universal qualities of business experience.

Now that you understand values, let's move on to events.

An event is when something happens. As McKee writes,

> *"A story event creates meaningful change in the life situation of a character." [Think company, if you like].*

In other words, something *happens*. And you can bet it's not, "We have a new product and here's what it does." Nor is it, "We're better than the competition." You can find all sorts of ways to use that information, but if you want to build a memorable story, events matter.

So what's "meaningful change?" Think back to those story values we were discussing. Going from "incapable" to "capable," shifting from "stagnant" to "innovative," leaping from "unknown" to "popular." You get the drift. An event, unrelated to a value, is not an event.

For instance, if Joe tells me, "We had a profitable quarter," that's not an event. It's a fact. Remember… one of those organized or disorganized facts that many people put into their non-stories.

But there could be a *value* associated with that fact, or maybe several. For instance, were we unprofitable for many quarters, with much fear of closure in the company, and concern about job loss? Had it been a company in despair that now found reason for new hope? Were people ready to leave the company until the announcement of a profitable quarter, and now there's a line of prospective candidates waiting to join? Now we're starting to build a story.

But that's not enough. McKee's full sentence goes on:

> *"A story event creates meaningful change in the life situation of a character [think, company] that is expressed and experienced in terms of a value and achieved through conflict."*

By now you understand there's no meaningful change without some value shift. And you understand that an event must represent some meaningful change. But conflict?

That's right. No conflict, no story.

You might be asking yourself how in the world you're going to introduce conflict into a business story. After all, there's no conflict in profitability or lack of profitability. There's no conflict in going from unknown to becoming a household name, from failure to success. Is there *any* conflict in business?

NEWS FLASH: THERE'S ALWAYS CONFLICT, AND CONFLICT MAKES GOOD STORIES

Imagine a highly innovative but unprofitable company. The board has been fighting with the brilliant, inspired, and impossible-to-deal-with CEO. Finally the board gets rid of him.

- Value shifts: profitable/unprofitable, loyalty/betrayal, working/unemployed
- Event: board fires CEO
- Conflict: between the CEO and board, but there could be others in this story. The CEO and his or her spouse, the Board and its shareholders, the CEO and employees, or the employees and the board.

Continuing our story: After firing the CEO, the company sees its sales drop precipitously over the next few quarters. The board doesn't know what to do.

- Value shifts: again, profitable/unprofitable (or hope/despair)
- Event: company reports bad numbers
- Conflicts: pick one – infighting among board members, management difficulties, engineering despair, employee malaise

Begrudgingly, the company hires back the former CEO. He makes a tough deal with the board members.

- Value shifts: profitable/unprofitable, hope/despair, right/wrong… pick one
- Event: CEO returns
- Conflicts: fight for leadership, disputes between board and CEO… pick one among many

Now the company comes back from the brink of disaster. In fact, under the returned CEO's leadership, it becomes one of the most innovative, respected and profitable companies in the world.

- Value shifts: failure/success, floundering/directed, average/top-notch
- Event: CEO leads company to the top
- Conflicts: making change in company culture, numerous staffing changes, fighting with board

We have just described, in an unfairly abbreviated format, the extraordinary story of Apple Computer. Are you reading this on an iPhone, iPad or other iDevice? Did the acquisition of that device constitute an event that you can talk about through a change in value and achieved through conflict? For some of us, buying a new device might involve some conflict with a spouse, a salesperson, our employer's purchasing department, a friend who said Apple products are a rip-off and that you'll get more power out of another type of tablet computer.

Many of us have devices on our person or desks about which there are events that can be expressed through shifts in values and which came about through conflict.

As we worked on this book, one team member pulled out his iPhone. He told about how he secretly got the newest model without telling his wife. He described getting home the evening he purchased the phone and then hearing his wife ask, "Can I borrow your phone, I forgot mine?" She never did this... but he had bought the new phone that day. He was planning to play with it after she went to bed. But instead, he had to pull it out of his pocket and hand it over.

Imagine the gap between her expectation – the cheap folding clamshell phone he used to carry – and the result. Imagine the ensuing conflict and the eventual change in value for his wife: from having an old iPhone to a new one!

But let's get back to business. Conflict presents one of the great challenges for many business storytellers. Sometimes it's hard to ferret out, and other times it can cause you to wonder if you really want to make it public. But in case you're thinking about conflict narrowly, take note:

CONFLICT ISN'T JUST BETWEEN PEOPLE

Most of us think of conflict as happening only between people, in other words personal conflict. There are three types of conflict, of which personal conflict isn't always the most important:

- Personal conflict, of course, is usually between people: the detective's commanding officer takes away his badge and his gun just when he needs them most. Or the captain, above that superior officer, fires the detective, but it's all a façade because he is the criminal and has put the hero cop in a deadly position.

- Then there's inner conflict, such as the conflict that occurs in your own mind when wrestling with priorities, ambitions, or desires. Consider your favorite cop movie. Most likely, there's a hero who deals with crippling inner conflict. He wrestles with his addiction to alcohol and his desire for a relationship with an ex-wife or girlfriend who dumped him because of the drinking.
- Finally, extra-personal conflict, such as conflict against conventional wisdom, social institutions, the weather or other conditions. For example, the detective's old car, which gives up just when he's near catching the murderer… and then it begins to storm.

Any number of the *Dirty Harry* movies rely on these and other conflicts as vehicles for significant change.

BUT CONFLICT IN BUSINESS?

You bet. Consider:

- Inner conflicts: the entrepreneur who has to balance responsibilities to her family with the desire to pursue a business idea and invest time and money, both of which are scarce in her life given a new child and a husband who walked out on her. Or the CEO who deals with an inner demon, causing him to gamble with his company's fate. The heir to a family business who decided to take his family company in a new direction and had to deal with a resistant board of directors, a vengeful family, and a boat-load of guilt and doubts.
- Personal conflicts: These abound in business – where there are often as many points of view as there are owners or managers.

- Extra-personal conflicts: economic conditions, market conditions, customer experiences, product failures, competitors, national crises, political changes, environmental considerations, unions… the list is endless.

When human beings join forces to create an enterprise – especially a business where livelihoods depend on success – conflicts will surface in every shape and size.

WHY EVENTS IN GOOD STORIES REQUIRE CONFLICT

Imagine a marketing manager, Bill, goes to work and his boss Melinda calls him into her office.

"I need to see a new version of 'that' press release," she says.

With a sinking feeling in his gut, Bill remembers "that" press release. It's the one about layoffs that she told him to draft. That was a few months ago, and she said it would never happen, but "we just need to be prepared."

We have a change in values – from Bill happily walking into the office to unhappily being told to dust off the layoff announcement. Suppose Bill had been anticipating layoffs and had been talking about it for months openly within the company. The value change would be smooth, expected, and life would go on as usual. There would be a change, but no conflict. No story.

Now suppose that Bill was told yesterday that things were looking good for the company. Higher than usual profitability, combined with increased customer interest, resulted in management considering expansion of production and facilities. In fact, just yesterday Bill had been told to draft and send a memo to all employees asking if anyone knew competent people who might join the team. And because of the optimism he perceived, he told a bunch of his friends that layoffs were put on hold indefinitely.

Do you see it building? Suddenly we have that "gap between expectation and result," combined with a value change, and clearly there's about to be some conflict:
- Conflict between Bill and Melinda about what he had been lead to believe

- Personal conflict inside Bill about what to do next, who to tell, whether or not to try to change the course of what's about to happen, and even whether or not his own job might be at stake. Does he start working on his resumé or work even harder for the company, hoping he's not let go?
- External conflicts, possibly within the company, with the external community or with shareholders

What stories might be told about this? Perhaps a division manager defies management to keep his staff – he works them 24/7 to produce a new product that becomes a showpiece for the company, and the company is saved – with all employees getting their jobs back.

Perhaps Bill, for the first time in his life, walks into the CEO's office and helps to change the course of history for all his fellow employees? Or perhaps he starts gathering co-workers to garner forces for a management buyout.

"A story event creates meaningful change in the life situation of a character [think, company] that is expressed and experienced in terms of a value and achieved through conflict." Starting to make sense?

Let's look at how events, shifts in value and conflict came together to help one business create compelling and memorable stories.

THE STORY OF TERRACLIME GEOTHERMAL

We got to know Terraclime Geothermal as it sought to create a new name. After an intensive process with the client, HB Agency came up with the name Terraclime, and under that name the company has become a regional leader in the New England geothermal market. Doug McVey, Terraclime's CFO, told us about the stories his business encounters every day.

"The homeowner's market is full of that 'gap between expectation and result.' People get into a house, and they dream about what they will do to it, how they will live in it, and how perfect their lives will be. Then they start seeing all the things that are really wrong – how they need to replace windows, re-do floors, deal with mold and mildew, repair the roof, fix sinks and bathrooms and furnaces… one of the biggest gaps happens with variable-cost items, like energy costs. Many people who bought homes when fuel oil was under two dollars per gallon have seen the price double, and with it a doubling of their winter heating costs. That's a huge change. And boy can you imagine stories happening in those homes, with meaningful changes in people's life situations, huge value shifts and enormous conflict.

"The story of our business is very much about constantly shifting values in our market. Every time the price of oil goes down, our whole country heaves a sigh of relief, homeowners feel better about their variable costs… and then the price goes up. New technologies are announced, and people get hopeful. Then those new technologies turn out not as great as people thought and more expensive. Despair settles in. Then there's another technological breakthrough, or the price of oil goes down, or there's a government incentive to buy new energy-producing technology…

"With homeowners beaten down by high and unpredictable heating and cooling costs, they face all sorts of conflicts. Should they move to a smaller house? Should they call the oil company to ask why the bill rose so much? Should they buy ahead at a fixed rate but suffer reduced cash flow? And then talk about interpersonal conflicts – think about the arguments most homes have around thermostat settings… what couple doesn't argue about that?

"In this landscape, our company steps in and helps people cut their energy bill 80% and their imported energy by over 90%.

"We used to tell customers about features and benefits. Now we tell stories that sound more like this:

"Tom Adams felt privileged to live in his family's old New England home – the home where he and his siblings had been raised, and two blocks away from his parents' new house. He and his wife Julie loved the house and the convenience of raising their own children so close to Tom's family, but they were spending more than they could afford on heating every winter. Not only did he worry about money, but it made Tom angry to think of his money going to foreign countries – not only providing jobs outside the US, but also putting our national security at risk. Julie had other reasons for her growing dislike of the house. She felt it was ill-equipped to deal with the more extreme weather that was happening every year – often they were too cold or too hot. They argued frequently, and the house was becoming a sore spot for both of them. He got angry when she turned up the air conditioning in the summer. And when she turned up the heat in the winter, he would turn it back down and tell her to put on another sweater.

"Tom looked at solar and wind, but the return on investment would take decades. As a last resort, he looked at geothermal.

"Unfortunately, Tom's wife made it clear that they couldn't afford a geothermal system. They argued about it for weeks, and in the end, school bills won out over changing their heating and cooling systems. Tom was about to call and tell us that it wouldn't work out when he opened the newspaper and read about federal incentives for residential renewable energy systems. Then he called his bank, and he found out that with the incentives and a loan, his yearly payments would actually be less than they currently paid for oil. In addition, they would be adding tremendous value to their house and living much more comfortably.

"Now he doesn't protest when his wife turns up the heat, and she doesn't mind when he uses the AC. What's amazing is they didn't even have central air before, just window units – so they get more light in the house and better ventilation when they choose to open their windows."

BUT THIS STORY IS ABOUT TOM AND JULIE, NOT TERRACLIME GEOTHERMAL!

Wrong. The hero in this story is Terraclime. But it's far more compelling to talk about Terraclime through the lens of a customer's story than through a boring discussion about technology, features and benefits. For a homeowner hearing this story, the point is "with the incentives and a loan, [Tom's] yearly payments would actually be less than they currently paid for oil." But without the story, that sounds like a sales pitch. With the story, it's not only compelling and memorable, but also a great call to action.

CHAPTER 4

AND THEN CAME CHARACTERS!

Or did they come first? Kurt Vonnegut says that every story must "give the reader at least one character he or she can root for," and that "every sentence [in a story] must do one of two things – reveal character or advance the action."

Remember:

> *"A story event creates meaningful change in the life situation of a character [think: company] that is expressed and experienced in terms of a value and achieved through conflict."*

We added "think: company" as we introduced you to this concept. But a business – in fact, any organization – is just the sum of the people who make it run, who interact with it, who sell for it and buy from it. There is no such thing as a business separate from the people in it and the people it serves.

This applies even in what we call the "B2B" or business-to-business world. We've helped hundreds of business-to-business companies fine-tune their messaging and produce marketing campaigns to fuel their growth. It has always amazed us to hear from CEOs and their teams, "Our customers are businesses; they don't respond to marketing." Or, "Our customers are engineers; they only care about features and benefits."

Whether they're engineers or school administrators, CEOs or stay-at-home parents, your customers are people. The same is true of your employees, board members and other stakeholders. And people relate most strongly to other people. Therefore, people must play the central roles in your most memorable and compelling stories.

PEOPLE RELATE TO PEOPLE.

This is why news stories almost always begin with an anecdote about a person as the introduction to a larger theme.

> *Marybeth Lansing could no longer afford her medications. Despite a good job as a factory worker where the company*

*paid most of her insurance coverage, Ms Lansing had a cap
on her prescription medication coverage. Given a chronic
back condition and expensive painkillers, her prescription
coverage usually ran out by September of each year.*

*Like many other workers with employer-sponsored insurance
plans...*

Such a story might go on to explain the problem, note the players
and arguments on different sides of the issue, and then return to
Marybeth's story at the end. Perhaps it would conclude with a
hopeful tale of how she has managed to make ends meet, or a more
hopeless description of how her retirement savings have dwindled
given her annual medication expenses.

The story about prescription medication coverage policy would
lose much of its power without Marybeth's personal anecdote. Most
readers will remember her story as the centerpiece around which
they will arrange their understanding of the issue.

Think back to the business stories used as examples in the first
three chapters of this book. In the Apple story, the central character
was not the business, but the CEO who left and returned. In the
L.L.Bean anecdote, the person abusing L.L.Bean's return policy
caught our attention. In the Terraclime Geothermal story, the
customers – Tom and Julie Adams – kept our attention because of
their drama, not the features and benefits of a geothermal heating
and cooling system. In these stories, *the meaningful change in the
life situations of a character, expressed and experienced in terms
of a value and achieved through conflict,* served to illustrate the
meaningful change that's happening to the business, or more
significantly, the meaningful change that the business can create for
its customer.

LEADERSHIP MATTERS, BUT ISN'T EVERYTHING.

Many businesses create or leverage stories about their leaders, but unfortunately not always because leaders have the best stories. Sometimes they do, and sometimes they have enormous egos, want their stories told, and no one around them has the courage to suggest it's a bad idea.

Steve Jobs (Apple Computer), Jack Welch (GE), John Mackey (Whole Foods Market), Bill Gates (Microsoft), Warren Buffett (Berkshire Hathaway), and many more business leaders have compelling stories. Their extraordinary success alone makes us want to know them. And at some point, success and fame overcome the need for a story to be compelling or memorable. Consider Bill Clinton's best-selling autobiography, *My Life*. Many of us bought it. Some of us read it. A few of us even finished it, despite its extraordinary length. But even without reading his autobiography, many people knew Clinton-related stories, often retelling them because they impressed, shocked or astonished. We even saw him as a great storyteller, given his riveting speeches and interviews. But the book... well, neither a compelling nor memorable read – we found ourselves amazed at the volume of detail he recalled even from his days as a small child. At the same time, we thought many times, "Why is he writing this part?"

For better or worse, most of us don't benefit from fame, infamy or widely recognized success, and our businesses do not have the cachet of Apple Computer or Whole Foods Market. We do not have Bill Clinton's personal and political capital to exploit when putting our stories into a crowded and noisy market. But we do have a business, customers, prospects, and a host of stories that could serve as rocket fuel for the next phase of our business' growth.

LEVERAGE YOUR COMPANY'S LEADERS, BUT DON'T LET IT BECOME TOO MUCH OF A GOOD THING.

We worked with a company in the environmental space that came to us to publicize one of its divisions and garner positive media exposure for its technology products. The leader of this division, let's call him Stu, impressed us with his acumen, his experience, and his ability to talk. And talk. And talk. Each of our meetings, which invariably lasted twice as long as planned, was filled with 70-80% of Stu talking, often about himself and his accomplishments.

One day Stu asked our opinions about a video he had envisioned for his company. We thought this was a great idea – most people enjoy consuming information through video, which is one reason why YouTube is the second most popular search engine in the world.

We had already reached out to a few media people who would be interested in writing about the company, and at times our employees had difficulty encapsulating the technology in a conversation. Video would allow us to show, not tell, a story about Stu's products and services and the difference they make for the company's customers.

Stu described his vision of the video:

"I envision the camera following me on my motorcycle as I drive to work. I'm wearing black leathers and a helmet, so you can't see my face yet, can't see that I'm the CEO." He gave a knowing smile, as if we all could understand how exciting it would be for viewers, how

{ **There's no way around it: people must play the central roles in your most memorable and compelling stories.**

they would wonder, *who is that masked man on the motorcycle?*

Stu continued: "I park the motorcycle, get off, remove my helmet. Now the audience knows it's me. The camera follows me into the office, where I greet people, check in on what they're up to… then it follows me to a meeting, where I interact, help solve some challenges…"

Eventually Stu wrapped it up, concluding: "You see… a day in the life of the CEO… what do you think?"

While Stu's company is growing and should be proud of its accomplishments, perhaps Stu envisioned himself as a bit too much of a superstar (ya think?). If he had been a performer or political figure whose fans wanted to know every detail, such a strategy might have been effective. Or if he had been CEO of a large public company, where many audiences wonder about the man at the helm… But as the CEO of a small technology subsidiary of a larger environmental firm, there was little reason to make a video about "The day in the life of…"

We responded with little enthusiasm, but tried to be diplomatic. While this might not be the best idea for a video, we didn't want to abandon the idea completely. Stu's customers cared about how his technology solutions would help them. They cared about him as an expert who could address his industry's challenges and opportunities. That has nothing to do with a play-by-play description of his daily routine. But it can make a great video.

What was missing from the video story Stu described?

Story events. He described a video where there were no value changes and certainly no conflict… nothing happened! That's not a story. It's a diary, and because Stu isn't a superstar, nobody cares.

There are two problems here: First, Stu might not be the best character to use in the story, and second, there was no story.

Now Stu's company could use him in a different way. But let's put that aside for a moment and consider all the potential "characters" and all the potential stories that a business creates. Employees, customers, partners, board members, members of the public, political figures, analysts, researchers, regulators, etc. The most important? Customers and employees, of course. But that doesn't mean you can't use some of the others now and again.

So how do I choose what characters to focus on?

You don't... yet. Before choosing which characters might be best for your story, it's important to think about who the story is designed to reach and influence.

In the environmental firm's case, Stu should have asked himself: Is this video story for employees, prospects, customers, stockholders or even regulators? If he had figured that out, he would have come a long way toward figuring out who should star in the video.

Stu eventually told us that he felt his story would inspire employees. "They want to know and understand their leader," he said. He was on the right track: Employees often want to learn more about their leader, looking to him or her for inspiration and guidance. But they're not interested in discovering their leader is a show-off. Or how beautiful his children are. Or what movie stars he met on vacation. These things might add color to the story, but they should not be the main components.

But leaders don't really show off like that, do they?

Unfortunately, we've met too many business leaders who seem to live for the opportunity to show off to their colleagues and employees.

Stu offered us one perspective on this. But in his case, he still could have used video as an effective communication tool to tell stories that really matter to his employees and/or prospects.

Imagine that he had used a video story as a teaching vehicle, going on a site visit and having the camera follow him as he explained the challenges and solutions in a customer's installation. It would be easy to work in a "story event" during the filming... perhaps Stu meets a customer who has been difficult to deal with and who is experiencing a tough challenge with the company's technology. He could set that up by talking to the camera and create instant tension about his upcoming meeting. What would happen?

How would the customer react to seeing Stu? Would they work together, or would the customer complain and then tell Stu to take back his company's product? How would expectation match result, would there be conflict, and would there be meaningful change expressed through a value change and achieved through conflict?

In terms of a value shift, it would be compelling to see Stu and his team bring a customer from dissatisfaction to satisfaction, and with that change, bring the relationship from strained to congenial.

We often shy away from conflict, but imagine the power of that video story if Stu could pull it off. What if he chose a customer that all employees knew as a particularly difficult customer, someone nobody wants to deal with? Such a video story would satisfy numerous objectives:

- Teaching employees conflict-resolution techniques
- Showing the boss as involved and capable
- Putting the boss "in the ranks," right there with employees who have to deal with difficult customers and situations
- Creating a memorable and compelling story that employees could easily retell

And that's just from the employee perspective. Stu's company could edit and release the video externally and create a fantastic customer story for a broader audience. Perhaps the formerly angry customer would become even more loyal and proud of his story on Stu's company website.

Finally, such a story would say a great deal about the company's leadership by revealing Stu's character. Robert McKee notes that:

> "...the character of a person is revealed by the choices she makes under pressure."

Does someone run for her life or save the dog when the house is burning? Does she tell an old man that he dropped a $100 bill or quietly pick it up and slide it into her pocket? Does the shift captain reach into the sewer to fix the pump or order an employee to do it while he watches? Does the commanding officer lead his troops from in front or behind?

In our vision of Stu's story, his character – or part of it, at least – is revealed when he chooses to confront an angry customer and make the situation right. Seeing that story, or reading it, his audience might well assume that his drive to do the right thing trickles down to the whole company.

Many of us have compelling stories around bad experiences we've had with certain vendors or suppliers. We also have stories about companies that turned a bad experience around and turned us into loyal customers. We tell these stories repeatedly, and they spread through word of mouth. Why then do so few businesses leverage such experiences in their marketing? Perhaps they're afraid that customers will take advantage of their desire to "do the right thing?" If so, they should look to L.L.Bean for leadership!

CHAPTER 5

GET EXTREME

Use the following space to jot down – quickly – some of the best stories you remember and have re-told. If you can confine it to business-related stories, great. If not, that's okay too. (If you don't want to write in this book, use a pad of paper. But we suggest writing directly in the book. You're reading this book to learn something, and the simple act of writing can help solidify new learning in your mind.)

_____

_____

_____

_____

_____

_____

_____

_____

_____

If you're like most people, your story examples included some extreme situations or behavior. We polled a number of people on what they remembered most vividly from three movies:

1. *Bridesmaids*: The bridal shop scene where the bride and her bridesmaids suffer from food poisoning
2. *Star Wars* series: The scene where Luke finds out Darth Vader is his father
3. *Rain Man*: The scene where Dustin Hoffman counts the toothpicks that have been dropped

In each of these examples, the story event sticks with us because it "goes all the way." Robert McKee would say it goes to the "limit of human experience."

The *Bridesmaids* scene starts with the bride and her bridesmaids in the most luxurious bridal shop in town and ends up in that same shop's sumptuous powder room with one bridesmaid jumping up on the sink because all the toilets are taken by her vomiting friends. As she yanks up her skirt and wriggles onto the sink to relieve herself, her friend looks up from vomiting in the toilet and shouts, "What are you doing?" In response, she screams "Look away, look away!"

In *Star Wars*, Luke fights Darth Vader. As the fighters move onto a dangerous bridge over empty space, lightsabers whirring, Vader swings and cuts off Luke's hand. The hand and Luke's lightsaber fly into the empty space below, buffeted by wind. Luke clings to the bridge as Vader implores him to join the Dark Side. Then Vader tells him, "I am your father."

In *Rain Man*, Raymond Babbitt, played by Dustin Hoffman, and his brother Charlie Babbitt, played by Tom Cruise, stop at a diner for lunch. Charlie grows frustrated with Raymond and his autistic mannerisms. But during their stop, Raymond reveals that he has read and memorized the phone book up to the letter G. By the end of the scene, as they are leaving, the waitress gives Raymond a box of toothpicks because he has been asking for one incessantly. The box spills and Charlie is once again annoyed at an unnecessary delay. Raymond says, "82, 82, 82," and Charlie tells him there are way more than 82 toothpicks. Raymond says, "Three times 82 is 246." Charlie finds out there are 250 toothpicks in the box, and says, "pretty close." Then the waitress looks up from the near-empty box that she has just picked up and tells him there are four remaining toothpicks in the box.

Each of these scenes pushes the limit of human experience. It would have been enough for the bridesmaids to all get sick, even to throw up. But defecating in the sink brings it to a whole new level. *Rain Man* drives home the message of Raymond's extraordinary cognitive abilities with the phone book memorization. The dramatic illustration with the toothpicks drives it home even further, topping one impossible feat with one that seems even more difficult in the moment. That scene also includes conflict because Charlie initially thinks Raymond didn't get it right and judges him for it. In the *Star Wars* example, Luke could simply have lost the fight or could have heard the news that Vader was his father in any number of other ways… yet he loses the fight to his father, who cuts off his hand and reveals himself as Luke clings to a metal rail, precipitously balanced above hundreds of feet of empty space. Admittedly, our business

> **But we can strive to bring life to our stories, pushing ourselves to be brave and seek the limit of each situation.**

stories will rarely provide fodder for such emotionally charged moments. But we can strive to bring life to our stories, reminding ourselves to be brave and pushing the limit of each situation.

How do we do this?

Let's go back to Terraclime Geothermal. Here's how we described the situation between Tom and Julie Adams:

"Tom Adams felt privileged to live in his family's old New England home – the home where he and his siblings had been raised, and two blocks away from his parents' new house. He and his wife Julie loved the house and the convenience of raising their own children so close to Tom's family, but they were spending more than they could afford on heating every winter. Not only did he worry about money, but it made Tom angry to think of his money going to foreign countries – not only providing jobs outside the US, but also putting our national security at risk. Julie had other reasons for her growing dislike of the house. She felt it was ill-equipped to deal with more extreme weather that was happening every year – often they were too cold or too hot. They argued frequently, and the house was becoming a sore spot for both of them. He got angry when she turned up the air conditioning in the summer. And when she turned up the heat up in the winter, he would turn it back down and tell her to put on another sweater."

At this point we must repeat… and focus in on the small type:

> *"A story event creates meaningful change in the life situation of a character that is expressed and experienced in terms of a value and achieved through conflict."*

One of the ways we register meaningful change is when a story pushes the limits of human experience. A wife yelling at her husband because he turns on the air conditioning, and a husband turning down the heat… these are not actions that approach any limit. The values "cold/warm" and "getting along/arguing…" approach only the milk toast of daily life.

But if we really dig, are there values at stake that have far greater impact for the Adamses? Such values would not only help the audience relate but would grab our attention and pull us into Tom and Julie's story, rooting for a good outcome.

Let's give it a try:

Tom had to choose between his childhood home and his wife, but couldn't make that choice.

He and his wife Julie kept the thermostat low to save money in winter, but their kids got sick more often and their colds lasted longer. This led to more absenteeism and put both Tom and Julie's jobs in jeopardy.

Mildew problems got worse in the hot and humid months because they didn't want to spend money on air conditioning, and consequently one of the children's asthma went out of control. They could barely count the number of visits they made to the ER, and they both hated to see their little girl using a steroid inhaler on a regular basis.

Julie felt that the only way forward might be a divorce, seeing how Tom would do everything, including living in a freezing house, to stay in his childhood home.

Now we're talking about major health issues and life choices, including divorce. Suddenly, Tom and Julie's story reaches more extreme limits of experience. What if an aging grandparent lived in the house, a grandparent whose well-being depends on cooling in summer and heating in winter?

Granted, it's a business story about a customer. But look deeply and you'll be surprised at how many businesses touch their customers' lives in deep and meaningful ways. Could Terraclime Geothermal be saving lives, or at least saving homes and marriages? Could your business?

ACHIEVED THROUGH CONFLICT

It's worth spending a little more time on "achieved through conflict." We've covered this briefly, but it bears remembering that human beings don't show much interest in stories where change doesn't happen through conflict. If our political representatives and parties got along famously, we would probably ignore politics most of the time. The stories we tell and retell include conflict – customer stories, social stories, business stories and political stores – even though many important changes come about without conflict.

Meaningful business change often includes conflict, but we have to admit that sometimes the conflict cannot be publicized. However, as we demonstrate in the Terraclime Geothermal story, conflict abounds in the lives that make up a business' many constituents.

What about your business' customers, employees, board members, public or other stakeholders? For each, there must be changes experienced in terms of one or more value and achieved through conflict. And sometimes, the story and its conflicts don't have to be directly related to the company or its work. This book's primary author recently experienced one such story.

THE RABID FOX - NICOLAS' STORY

In the summer of 2011, I was enjoying my backyard with a handful of friends and their children. Late in the afternoon, I was in the pool with my son, my wife and my neighbor Jen, who had brought her three children. All in all, there were six five-year-old children playing in the shallow end of the pool.

I was away from the kids when I noticed my dog Bean trotting along the edge of the pool, closely followed by a mangy-looking fox nipping at her heels.

I knew something was wrong – I've seen foxes move, and this one looked sluggish and scruffy. Plus, I had never seen a fox come toward a crowd of people. They are skittish creatures, and it's a rare pleasure to see one in the flesh.

"Get away!" I screamed at the fox, but it simply kept trotting behind Bean, who ducked under the picnic table. Before I could get out of the pool, my wife had rushed out from the shallow end and jumped on top of the picnic table shouting at the animals. She meant to frighten the fox, but she scared Bean, who ran away into the bushes. The fox pursued Bean, and my wife pursued both of them. Suddenly all was quiet. I stepped out of the pool and searched for some sort of weapon in case the fox returned, while asking Jen and all the kids to stay in the pool for the time being. I figured that was the safest place.

Suddenly, the fox returned from the bushes alone and trotted toward me. I grabbed the closest thing I could find: a croquet mallet. The fox came at me, seemingly unconcerned with my weapon, so I tried to get away and jumped into the shallow end of the pool. The fox followed, then trotted along the edge of the pool looking as if it might jump in at any moment.

My adrenaline was pumping fast, and just as the fox came closest to me by the pool's edge, I raised the mallet and struck it on the head. The animal collapsed but kept moving, and I hit it again until it stopped. In fact, I kept hitting it to make sure it was dead. Then I heard the screaming. I turned around to see Jen with her arms around all the kids, trying to shield them from the massacre they were witnessing. The kids were screaming bloody murder. One girl was begging to go home, and a boy shouted out, "I want to go to New Hampshire," probably the farthest place he could imagine.

It turned out that the fox was rabid and had already bitten two people in town. It had even gone through a local pizza shop's kitchen and terrorized the staff.

But here's the most interesting thing: years later, I'm still known in my town for killing a rabid fox with a croquet mallet, even though few people saw the event. The story included all the elements of a good story: significant value shifts involving safety and risk, external conflict, internal conflict about killing an animal in front of children, and the potential for very meaningful change in the life of all the characters, should any of us have been bitten by the fox. It's a compelling and memorable story that quickly infiltrated my business life. My business partner emailed links to an article about the fox to a few key clients, and when I meet with them they still ask, "had any run-ins with a fox lately?"

While I believe I acted on instinct and got lucky with my shot (I've probably played croquet all of twice in my life), the story reflects my ability to take action when it's needed, to act with courage under pressure, to put myself at risk and to protect the people around me. It also shows the same about my wife. I believe that for some of my business relationships, the characteristics illustrated by the story help crystallize the reasons why people enjoy working with my company. While the story has nothing to do with my business… it somehow does.

SONS OF MAXWELL - DAVID BITES GOLIATH

A band is a business, and like most businesses, bands can range from "side business," such as wedding bands that play for fun and extra money on the weekend, to "mom and pop shop," where band members earn enough to put food on their tables but no more, to "multinational corporation," such as Eminem, the Rolling Stones or Shakira.

Sons of Maxwell, a Canadian band from Halifax, was known only by a small and loyal group of fans. Then they released the song "United Breaks Guitars."

The main story event occurred on March 31, 2008.

The band had boarded a plane to travel from Halifax to Omaha, Nebraska, on United Airlines, when someone sitting near Dave Carroll, the band leader said, "Look, they're throwing guitars out there." Carroll looked outside and saw that, indeed, the band's guitars were being carelessly tossed about by United's baggage handlers.

Carroll's guitar was broken when it arrived in Omaha, and Carroll spent the next few months dealing with United's customer service in hopes of getting some sort of compensation. When the discussion finally ended unsuccessfully, Carroll wrote the song, "United Breaks Guitars" and created a YouTube video to go with it. The song/video combination went viral, becoming an instant YouTube and iTunes hit and a PR disaster for United Airlines.

In interviews, Carroll says the band's website went from selling one or two CDs per week to hundreds, even thousands. The band received many more requests to play across the US, Canada and other countries. Carroll became an international folk sensation, appearing on talk shows and playing at venues that Sons of Maxwell would never have dreamed possible before the United incident.

Through it all, Carroll never changed his good nature and sense of humor, which is part of what helped him and his story grow so popular. He eventually wrote three songs chronicling the United incident. The last one forgives United and the customer service representative, Ms. Irlweg, who was only doing her job when enforcing United's policy and refusing to help with the guitar damage.

This story brings into play many of the concepts we have been discussing.

- Meaningful change in the life of the character: A musician's instrument broken, but more importantly, he and his band went from being relatively unknown to having a worldwide following.
- Change expressed and experienced in terms of a value: The musician was happily traveling to a gig and then became unhappy when looking out the window. More importantly, he then went from unhappily trying to work through United's customer service to happily enjoying unplanned success.
- Change achieved through conflict: The song that brought Carroll fame was actually written as part of his conflict with United.
- Pushing the limit: The title of Carroll's first song could have been "United Mishandles Luggage," but he called it "United Breaks Guitars." This detail alone is very important – the song title pulls us in much more dramatically than if he had gone softer with it.

Carroll engages in professional speaking, has published a book – with guess what title? *United Breaks Guitars* – and continues to play music with his band.

Businesses and the people who build them never cease to amaze us with their compelling stories. Even if your business isn't a band, and you haven't had the rotten luck of watching your guitars tossed around by luggage handlers, we know you have many great stories.

Stories like Dave Carroll's should inspire you, as should the story of Ben & Jerry, the ice-cream makers.

BEN & JERRY - DAVID PUMMELS GOLIATH

Early on in the company's life, as Ben & Jerry's Premium Ice Cream started gaining popularity in and around their home state of Vermont, founders Ben Cohen and Jerry Greenfield discovered that Pillsbury was strong-arming one of its distributors. The food giant told the distributor that it could either represent Pillsbury's brand Häagen-Dazs or Ben & Jerry's, but not both.

The ice-cream company mounted a PR campaign entitled, "What's the Dough-Boy Afraid Of?" This campaign from a small Vermont-based ice-cream maker brought the company national fame, including broadcast coverage, national news stories and a cover story in *Time Magazine*. Within months of that campaign, Ben & Jerry's ice cream was selling nationally, and soon after, internationally.

Again: meaningful value changes achieved through conflict. These are the stories that we find compelling and memorable and that influence the behavior of thousands of customers for these businesses.

They also illustrate the fact that although the popular saying goes, "sex sells," you can find many other things to stick in your customers' and prospects' minds.

CHAPTER 6

SEX SELLS, BUT FEAR STICKS

In his TED talk, "Abundance is our Future," Peter Diamandis, the Intel entrepreneur best known for being the founder and chairman of the X PRIZE Foundation, starts by showing news clips with gripping bad news collected over a six-month period: tornadoes, attacks, explosions, storms, bombs, disasters, etc. Diamandis then says:

The news media preferentially feeds us negative stories, because that's what our minds pay attention to. And there's a very good reason for that. Every second of every day, our senses bring in way too much data than we can possibly process in our brains.

And because nothing is more important to us than survival, the first stop of all that data is an ancient sliver of the temporal lobe called the amygdala. Now, the amygdala is our early warning detector, our danger detector. It sorts and scours through all of the information looking for anything in the environment that might harm us. So given a dozen news stories, we will preferentially look at the negative news. And that old newspaper saying, 'if it bleeds it leads,' is very true.

Stories that scare us grab our attention. Even our own scary stories linger in our consciousness. In fact, we often gleefully retell "never again" stories about risks we took or dangers we experienced. Even without knowing why, we understand such stories will captivate our audiences. And when we do the telling, we are rewarded by friends who pause with their forks hanging in the air, coworkers who gather to listen, relatives who invariably ask, "Then what happened? Did they get the alligator back into the cage?" Or, "Did the fox hurt your wife or dog when they all disappeared behind the hedge?"

But how do we manage the power of fear in business stories and in business marketing? After all, we don't want prospects or customers to be afraid of our company or products.

Consider nearly any pharmaceutical advertising. Some ads feature positive messages about what life could be without a particular condition or ailment… arthritis, allergies or erectile dysfunction. But many ads capitalize on our fears: for example, ads for anti-depressants that always show people alone, sighing, their head in their hands, clearly having a tough time. "You may suffer from [insert name of condition here]. Ask your doctor…"

Such ads or marketing tactics, and the incomplete stories they tell, take advantage of your need to ward off danger. That hard-wired need is so powerful that your brain fills in the story for you. You see the poor depressed patient suffering from name-your-chemical-imbalance, and you easily project yourself into that person's shoes. *I had a down day last week… am I unbalanced in this way? Am I hopeless and lost like that person?*

What could be more powerful? Sex? Sure, and we know that sex sells. But for most of us, it's a stretch to relate sex to our businesses. Fear is much less of a stretch, and possibly more effective. While we're not suggesting that you manufacture fear in relation to your products or services, we do think that you can tell stories about your business, your people or your customers and leverage the fact that your human prospects and customers are predisposed to respond to fear.

In the Terraclime story, we can identify with the fear of divorce, of losing a home, of a child growing unhealthy and of an elder suffering. Terraclime helps solve some of these challenges for its customers, and the story suggests that it can do the same for you. Even if you don't face those specific struggles, the story leverages some near-universal threats that a homeowner or parent might face. In this case, since the intended audience is a homeowner, the story raises the appropriate concerns for that audience.

Which brings us to audience. If you can understand your audience, you will also understand the right story to tell.

CHAPTER 7

AUDIENCE COMES FIRST
SECOND AND THIRD

If you were an artist, you would follow your muse, no matter how the audience responded. That's an artist's job, and it produces some of history's greatest innovations and disruptions. Sometimes we're shocked, turned off, turned on or simply bewildered by art, but generally we value the way art gets us thinking, talking, addressing the issues that inspire us or make us uncomfortable.

But you're not an artist. You're a CEO, CMO, marketing director or content strategist who cares about strategic communication. You work hard to make an impression and compel your audiences to action. Without those audiences, you don't have a job. So while you might have a muse that you want to follow, you take actions at work for other reasons – for business reasons. If you perform your job well, you get to enjoy long-lasting, rewarding relationships with your customers. Relationships illustrated by compelling, memorable stories.

Near the beginning of this book, we wrote:

"Compelling: This means that the story grabs your attention."

Then we discussed what we meant by "your." In part, we meant you (you can't tell a compelling story if you think the story's no good), but more importantly, we meant your audience. The same applies to memorable – it's great if you remember it. But frankly, you remember much more about yourself than your audiences ever will or should.

You know the people in your audience, and if you don't, you better figure it out quickly.

- Listen to them
- Speak to them
- Engage with them

What are they asking for? What do they care about?

	Bad Solution	Good Solution
Right Problem		
Wrong Problem		

Most of us have seen this table, which illustrates where we sometimes make our biggest mistakes – creating a good solution to the wrong problem (black square). Business stories often end up in that very square – they are good stories, but aimed at the wrong audience.

Remember Stu? If you're thinking his idea of himself on video made a bad story, you might be right... for you. But there's an audience for that story – an audience who might well have valued it: First of all, Stu seemed quite fond of it himself. You might laugh, but all of us fall into the *I like it so it must be good* trap. Second, people who are close to him and want to know more about him – his wife, his kids, his close friends – might have enjoyed the video.

The problem is that Stu was probably thinking, "I find these things interesting, so my employees and customers – in other words everyone – will find them interesting too."

Sometimes this happens during media buying, where a great ad will be featured at the wrong time or with the wrong programming or in the wrong medium. We generally figure that someone thought the show was right for the ad, but didn't bother to study the audience.

You can easily avoid such traps by considering your audience first. If Stu wants to inspire and influence his employees, then he might score a home run with a video featuring his work with a difficult client and how he brought about a great solution and created a stronger relationship. If he wants to impress customers, he might simply address a customer challenge that existed before his company got involved. Then he could show how he and his company fixed the problem.

By now you probably recognize that such a story would be expressed through a significant shift in values for the customer, from a difficult challenge to a working solution. But you might wonder where the conflict would happen – remember, we get more interested in stories where the significant change is brought about through conflict.

In this case the conflict could be on the customer side. She could experience internal conflict as she works through various competitive solutions and tries to pick the right company to work with. Or she could experience extra-personal conflict as her executive team starts to argue about different solutions to the problem. Perhaps there was already an investment in a mediocre solution, creating additional conflict. Remember, conflict is everywhere. You just need to uncover it.

No matter what, you must have your audience in mind when you decide what story to create and where to publicize it. For a business, you will generally be thinking about four main audience groups:

1. Customers
2. Employees
3. Investors
4. Industry-specific audiences: regulators, government, partners, etc.

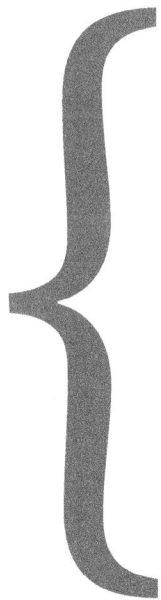

{ **No matter what, you must have your audience in mind when you decide what story to create and where to publicize it.**

5. Influencers (media, bloggers, tweeters, teachers, employers, analysts, authors, resellers, friends, family, advisors)

Note that each of these audience groups can be divided, depending on your market, into several sub-categories. For instance, customers might include different geographic, demographic or psychographic groups. Employees might be divided into different hierarchical or regional subsets.

THE DANGER OF ONE-SIZE-FITS-ALL

One of the quickest ways to generate lackluster, milk-toast stories is to create them for all your audiences in one package. Anything you create designed to target everyone will inspire, excite and compel
no one.

In our years working with businesses large and small, this is one of the most common mistakes. From a desire to please every internal stakeholder, marketing managers and executive teams produce stories that incorporate every perspective and end up having no effect on any of their constituent groups. What matters most to each audience segment is buried among details that don't matter to
that audience.

Figure out your audience, and create a story that's meant for that audience alone. Resist the temptation to add more details that might please other audiences or other stakeholders on your team. Your colleague or boss will invariably come along and say, "If we just tell a bit more about this other thing, then we can also use this story for another audience." Just say no! Your work will only suffer, and your audiences will only care less.

In the Terraclime Geothermal story, imagine if the idea was to impress a partner company who supplies copper tubing for the geothermal installations. To do this, the marketing team decides to put a two-minute segment in the video highlighting how the copper tubing is used in the installation and what a difference it makes over other kinds of tubing.

For the copper tubing supplier, this two-minute segment is buried in a story about Tom and Julie Adams, which is irrelevant to what the supplier cares about. For the residential prospect, the copper tubing segment not only interrupts the flow of Tom and Julie's compelling story, but it adds irrelevant information. Such information might lead to difficult questions such as, "Isn't copper more expensive than other types of tubing? Why do you use it?" Suddenly the focus has shifted from what the solution might do for the customer to a discussion about technical features that do nothing to advance the sales process.

That's not to say there isn't a place for a story about the copper tubing and why Terraclime uses it. Such a story might be designed for prospective customers who care about the technology. And it would include few, if any, details about Tom and Julie and their house.

Do your very best to create your stories for specific audiences. You will not regret the investment in thought and effort; besides, it's generally more difficult to create a story to please everyone.

CHAPTER 8

FROM CHILDHOOD TO
BUSINESS,
GOOD STORIES STICK

So now you understand key concepts for storytelling. As you read this book, keep your ears and eyes open to the stories that resonate with you in your own professional and domestic settings.

- Find the gaps between expectation and result
- See how character is revealed by choices made under pressure
- Notice events that create meaningful change in the lives of the characters
- Figure out how these events are expressed and experienced in terms of shifts in values achieved through conflict

Innumerable great stories adhere to these principles, including some stories you have known all your life – stories that seemed so simple that you never would have thought much of them...
until you looked.

IT STARTED WHEN YOU WERE A KID!

Consider "The Three Little Pigs." The characters: Helga, Marcel and Etienne – at least in some versions – start off as cute, innocent pigs who enjoy a happy existence at home with their mother.

Their mother tells them that they need to learn to live on their own, and she kicks them out. This creates a dramatic value shift for the pigs, from "comfy happy" to "cold without." They experience a massive gap between the expected evening at home and the resulting night on their own. The shift is achieved through conflict as their mother pushes them out the door despite their protests.

Out in the cold, another conflict awaits, one that might lead to an even bigger change in value: The big bad wolf will hunt the pigs down one by one, bringing them from safe to threatened and possibly from alive to dead.

Meanwhile the pigs wrestle with *inner* conflicts ranging from arrogance to carelessness, with *personal* conflicts as they disagree about what to do, and with *extra personal* conflicts that include the wolf and the weather.

The story provides several changes in values. For instance, after each pig builds a house to keep himself *safe*, he is then *threatened* when the wolf destroys his house. The sequence of events includes all the concepts we've discussed, and creates a story that takes the pigs from "kicked out of Mom's" to "happy in the brick house," with numerous stages in between.

The Little Engine That Could gives us another great example, with neither a threatening wolf nor a difficult mother.

The story starts with a change in value: An engine pulls a train of happy toys to the children in a town beyond the mountain. Suddenly, the engine breaks down. All the happy toys become sad and worried. Some cry.

Then, several engines roll by stopping to chat. Each one offers hope for a happy reversal of fortune. But one engine is too proud to help, one too old, and one too busy. Each time, the toys become *hopeful*, only to end up *disappointed*.

Finally, a little engine comes by, and (creating a huge gap between expectation and result) it decides to help despite its tiny size. We all know the rest of the story, and the mounting suspense as the engine climbs the mountain and puffs, "I think I can, I think I can, I think I can, I think I can."

Think back to your favorite childhood stories, and you will find numerous examples of the elements we have presented, even in the simplest, shortest stories you remember. Well, maybe not *Goodnight Moon*.

Can business stories really be made so simple, compelling and memorable?

We already mentioned Ben & Jerry's and the stories associated with L.L.Bean. We mentioned some of the companies we've helped over the years.

While we like to focus on smaller businesses, it's hard to ignore Tylenol's story, which still informs Johnson & Johnson's reputation thirty years later.

It was the fall of 1982. Seven unsuspecting users of the most popular over-the-counter drug in the United States, Tylenol, died after consuming cyanide-laced Tylenol tablets. Johnson & Johnson (J&J)'s team swung into action, determined to protect consumers from its #1 product. Unfortunately, that product accounted for 19% of J&J's profits in the first three quarters of 1982.

- Within a week of the first death, the company launched a massive PR campaign telling consumers not to purchase or use Tylenol
- The company pulled all of the product off shelves – 30 million bottles, at a cost of $100 million
- J&J redesigned Tylenol's manufacturing process and packaging
- The company voluntarily provided volumes of information to the public, and continued to offer sympathy for the victims (many companies would have let the story die as quickly as possible)
- Numerous other PR-related activities showed that J&J was also a partial victim of the crime while highlighting its corporate citizenship as a responsible, friendly and credible company

Within a short time, Tylenol gained back its market share and, arguably, more positive mindshare with consumers than it had before. How often was this story told and retold? In the media alone, over 125,000 news clips attest to the power of the negative story and the ensuing redemption story.

Obviously, the key event in this story is Tylenol's initial failure to prevent tampering with its bottles. Many of the greatest business stories include some sort of failure, like Tyco International and Enron. Such failures affect millions of people and gain worldwide media attention. And of course, they're not how the people who run businesses want to be remembered.

Interestingly, the stories of failures are often unrelated to the quality of their products and services or the features and benefits they offer every day. Sometimes a great story has nothing to do with your customers, your employees, or your management. Sometimes it has nothing to do with your products or services. Yet you can leverage other events, or ancillary people, products, and services to build your own stories.

BANZAI BURGER - LEVERAGING THE UNEXPECTED

Banzai Burger set up shop early in the summer of 2011, in a small whitewashed building on the thin strip of land leading out to East Hampton, a luxury summer community near the tip of Long Island.

The restaurant, offering a beach-like atmosphere, cocktails and a combination of American burgers and Japanese Sushi-bar food, got some good publicity and a warm greeting by the community when the season opened in early June. But it wasn't until July 15 that the community heard the story by which they would best remember the restaurant.

"We had a giant lobster statue that we called Kobe, which was seven feet long and weighed 500 pounds. His name was kind of a play on words given that we were serving great burgers. Kobe was promoting eating burgers and not his kind," said owner/manager Alex Duff. "On the night of July 14, Kobe was stolen from the front of the restaurant. Now, this is a big and heavy statue and probably difficult to hide. So we called the papers, and we ended up getting incredible coverage with headlines like "Giant Lobster Mascot Cruelly Stolen from Hamptons Restaurant." The story went viral and was covered by local TV, broadcast by Fox News and aired in three markets as well as being picked up in about 15 news items. Of all the things people could steal, this was surprising, if not extreme. And it put us in some jeopardy, because we felt it was one of the best means of getting people to look at the restaurant from the road – visible, different, and big. But it turned out well because the story of Kobe getting stolen and the resulting search was the introduction many people needed to check out the restaurant.

"The fact that we weren't interested in pursuing the thieves legally also revealed a lot about the restaurant's friendly atmosphere and management's commitment to being a positive force in the community [note how character is revealed by choices made under pressure]. We felt that if the thieves would only bring Kobe back, all would be forgiven.

"About six weeks later, when we had pretty much forgotten about Kobe, he reappeared on the side of the road roughly 4 miles away from the restaurant. The police were called and we were able to pick him up from the impound lot. We never found out who had done it, but we got another glut of publicity for that. I guess the thieves probably got tired of hiding a 500-pound lobster! Kobe still represents the restaurant, but from a much safer place away from the road in our new Sunset Lounge"

Does Banzai Burger's story get your wheels spinning? What stories do you have about your business, and how can they be leveraged to get positive attention and bring your customers and prospects to action? If you draw a blank when thinking about what great stories surround your business, you might turn to television as a source of inspiration. Commercials provide very short stories, and sometimes they can inspire us with extraordinary execution – getting a point across and creating a compelling, memorable experience at the
same time.

STORIES IN ADS

Advertising has become one of our great storytelling vehicles, and television commercials occasionally provide masterful stories in 30 seconds. Consider these four top commercials from 2011:

Nissan Leaf - Gas-Powered Everything

We find ourselves in a dirty, dystopian world. Everything, from blow-dryers to computers, is powered by a gasoline engine. A jogger inhales fumes from someone's cell phone. A woman pollutes her bathroom with thick exhaust from her blow-dryer. But at the end, the ad shows a crystal-clear, fume-free world featuring the Nissan Leaf.

- The values change is massive, from a dirty, noisy world where even the computer requires gasoline and exhaust fumes pollute every indoor and outdoor space to a spotless, glistening world where a driver pulls a cord from his Nissan Leaf and drives away silently

- We can easily identify with the characters: ordinary people looking slightly beaten-down, just making it through their lives… a man in the bathroom getting ready for work and dealing with the exhaust fumes from his wife's blow-dryer, a woman jogging through the exhaust fumes coming out of a pedestrian's cell phone, a regular Joe filling his computer with yellow gasoline from an office filling station that looks like a water cooler

While the final result, the "meaningful change" is not brought about by conflict, every scene shows conflict or potential conflict between characters and their gas-powered devices (some are not functioning), their environment, and at times each other as they use their noisy, dirty, exhaust-producing technology.

Snickers - Peanut Butter Squared
"Focus Group"

We're in a conference room and a woman asks, "Okay, so which one tasted better." She stands in front of two large pictures, one with an ordinary-looking man and another with a non-descript woman.

> **Commercials provide very short stories, and they can inspire us with their ability to move us in only a few seconds.**

Another voice starts in:

"Steve [interrupt from a third voice "Yeah, the guy"] – with Lisa I only tasted peanut butter and chocolate…" as he talks, the camera switches to the woman's point of view: a board room with four great white sharks sitting in the chairs, describing how the two people tasted. Turns out that with Steve, they tasted "something more… it was peanut butter and, uh… Snickers." He turns out to be right, as "Steve had just eaten Snickers Peanut Butter Squared." After a brief moment of discussing the deliciousness of Steve, given what he ate, one of the sharks says, "I'd love another taste."

The woman says "certainly," rings a buzzer, and a young man walks in eating one of the halves of a Peanut Butter Squared bar. One of the sharks says, "Eat both squares, please."

- Gap between expectation and results? Absolutely.
- Significant change expressed through a value shift… you bet.
- Conflict – understated, but understood!

Chrysler 200 – Born of Fire

Dark music and scenes of industrial Detroit put us in a tough American landscape: smokestacks and factories, tired neighborhoods and burned-out buildings. "What does a town that's been to Hell and back know about the finer things in life?" asks a gritty-sounding narrator. "It's the hottest fires that make the toughest steel," says the voice, as the camera glides around *Fist of a Champion*, the enormous sculpture of an arm and fist – a monument to Joe Louis in the heart of downtown Detroit.

The shiny black Chrysler 200 drives through town, its glistening windows reflecting scenes of a tough, run-down city with continued gritty narration. The car appears only fleetingly, until the end when a young man parks it and steps out to walk into the ornate and empty Fox Theatre. He wears a hooded sweatshirt. From the narration about the toughness of Detroit and the labor of that city's American workers, the sound switches to a beautiful gospel choir, which appears on stage in the empty theatre as the young man walks down the center aisle, hood over his head. It's Eminem, and he steps onto the stage, points into the camera, and says, "This is the Motor City, and this is what we do."

We see tremendous value shifts from the recession-worn city to the shiny new car, the gritty voice to the gospel singers… and in the car, not a middle-aged white man in business-casual clothes, as you might see in other luxury car commercials, but Eminem in a gray T-Shirt and black hoodie. The ad is rife with conflict, with the narrator alluding to what people have said about Detroit, to the fact that it's no New York City, or Windy City, or Sin City, "and we're certainly no one's emerald city." It tells a story of opposites, of hard work, of survival – one in which the car's driver, a street kid from one of the city's toughest neighborhoods, has made it further than most people and can easily afford whatever luxury he wants. Just like his talent, the car emerges from the city of steel.

Volkswagen - The Force

The commercial opens to Darth Vader theme music from *Star Wars*. A child in a Darth Vader costume strides through his house, cape flowing behind him, stopping in various places to try to move things with the force: He stretches out his arm and concentrates on exercise equipment, a dog lying on the carpet, the clothes washer, a doll on a bed… but nothing moves or changes. Then the child, still wearing the costume, is at the kitchen counter next to his mom. He uses his hands to try to summon his sandwich plate with The Force, but his mother slides it over instead. The child shakes his head in frustration and leans on his hand, elbow on the counter. We hear the sound of Dad's car pulling into the driveway. The dog barks. As Dad walks into the house, the child races past him. Dad gives a surprised glance at the little Darth Vader who doesn't even acknowledge him. The child takes a stand in front of Dad's car, stretches his hands forward and starts to work his magic. We can't help but remember Luke Skywalker summoning The Force to lift his X-wing fighter out of the swamp as Yoda looks on.

Suddenly, the car starts up. The child jumps back, shocked, but thrilled. Dad stands at the kitchen window with Mom and has just pushed the remote start. The child looks around in astonishment, looks back at the car, and straightens up. The Darth Vader music kicks into full force.

In one minute, using neither dialogue nor special effects, this commercial tells a compelling story – one that garnered over 52 million views in its first year on YouTube. The story is clear – the child's frustrations building up until he tries one last time – and his frustration turns to shock and joy. As a viewer, in only one minute, you're sucked into the child's palpable shift from the fantasy of power to the realization of powerlessness, and finally to the ultimate sense of empowerment. To add color to the story: When the mother slides over the sandwich with her hand – the sandwich he was unable to move with the force, her look shows both annoyance and compassion. This shifts to joy when she looks out the window and sees her child's delight at starting the car.

And of course we don't need to delve into each bit of conflict – suffice it to say that the idea of conflict happens with every object the child faces, and even his mother at the moment when she is slightly annoyed.

Most of us cannot afford the agencies, actors and budgets of such ads. But remember surprise and incongruity from Shakespeare? Remember the idea of a gap between expectation and result, value shifts, meaningful change brought about through conflict? Each of these commercials leverages these concepts to engage the audience in the story. They end up both compelling and memorable.

You don't need big budgets to build your stories with the concepts we have discussed.

STORIES IN VIDEOS:

Businesses-promoting video stories have become ubiquitous on YouTube, Vimeo and corporate websites. A quick search will show you an enormous number of videos, some of which benefit from big budgets, some of which don't, but the most memorable of which tell compelling stories.

For example, check out the "3M Corporate Video" uploaded by 3M Food Safety to YouTube. This "look at us" video features a montage of images and text, showing the breadth and depth of the company's innovations, continuing R&D and deployed products in numerous industries. But like the stock soundtrack that repeats innumerable times, the video becomes tiresome after 60 seconds of its 3:19 length. Products, services, and innovations galore... all very impressive, but none of it would make dinnertime conversation. And a few minutes after watching, it's difficult to remember any of the content. We watch this video, and we learn a bit more about 3M, possibly remembering that the company plays in products and industries we had not expected.

As an alternative, consider the video, "The Emotional Story of Reddit's Start & Sale" posted on Inc.com. The video is longer than 3M's, at 3:31, and features only Alexis Ohanian talking about starting Reddit, and how in the midst of the crazy startup time he received a call about his mother who had been diagnosed with terminal brain cancer.

When he spoke to his mother following the diagnosis, her first words were, "I'm sorry," as if somehow she had failed him by having terminal cancer.

Ohanian describes how his work became more about his mother, about showing that her efforts in raising him had come to something. And he describes how she was the first person he called after Condé Nast purchased Reddit – before calling any of the investors or media who were waiting to find out what happened.

The only line about Reddit's function appears at the beginning of the video with the following text in black on a white background: "In 2005, Alexis Ohanian and his best friend Steve Huffman created the 'front page of the internet.'"

In an informal experiment of 15 people watching both videos, only one went on to 3Ms website after watching its corporate video. Nine went on to Reddit's website after watching the Alexis Ohanian video. Two days later, all 15 people remembered specific details about Ohanian's story and remembered the name "Reddit."

This mirrors our experience of telling the rabid fox story to some of HB Agency's clients and friends. While Ohanian weaves his personal story into his business story, the fox story has absolutely nothing to do with the business. Yet it shows that even so, a "memorable and compelling" story about someone in the business can leave a lasting positive impression with your target audiences.

STORIES IN DIRECT MARKETING PIECES:

In her Ted Talk, "Design to Challenge Reality," designer Kelli Anderson describes a holiday greeting card she created for her friends. When you open the card, you can bend it in different ways to reveal a sequence of four different images: first, an image of the card, followed by the card being mailed, the envelope being opened, and finally an image of the card held in someone's hand. As Anderson puts it, the recipient interacts with "literally a four-frame documentary about opening the card."

Direct marketing offers rich opportunities to tell stories that might impact our recipients. Most of us think of direct mail as

{ **The opponent doesn't have to be a person. Think of it as an opposing force.**

"junk mail," because it often goes from our hand to the wastebasket without a second look. But if you have customers or prospects you want to reach and influence, taking the time to expose your recipient to a compelling and memorable story through some sort of dimensional mailer can offer a terrific return on investment.

Take HB Agency's client Aquanima, for example. The CEO wanted to reach C-level executives at banks of a certain size in North America – banks with 300 branches or more. Such banks had generally grown organically and through acquisitions and often failed to consolidate their spending. In other words, different branches used different suppliers for similar services, leaving great opportunities for consolidation and spend optimization.

Aquanima could save banks millions or even tens of millions of dollars, and it had done so throughout Europe and Latin America. Given recent successes with one US bank, the CEO knew he was in a strong position to help others that fit the profile. In fact, he believed that if he could get a one-on-one conversation with a target bank's CEO or CFO, he would close a deal. He hoped to have five such conversations over two years, and close one or two deals.

The company had contemplated a PR strategy to garner name recognition among North American financial institutions. A few articles in the right publications, coupled with the right speaking engagements, might indeed win some visibility among the targeted financial institutions. However, we believed that instead of investing in a year or two of PR, an equal or less budget could be invested in a high-impact direct outreach to accelerate results. We combined a visually arresting package, a direct-calling campaign and an online presence to reach out to the target executives.

While the package included several components, it leveraged stories of banks that were getting squeezed by unmanageable and unpredictable costs, poor spending infrastructure and lower profitability than they would have liked. These stories focused on the top executives and how they defined success.

The package itself symbolized a life-changing event. The box's clean, uncluttered look offered a breath of fresh air coming into the busy CEO's office. Opening it, there were only three short documents and a foam insert with a cutout space. In that space lay a cell phone, fully charged and pre-programmed to dial the CEO of Aquanima.

We knew that our target audience lived the "bank-CEO story" every day – exceedingly busy, focused on the bottom line, and putting out fires. The few words we used in the package made it clear that we knew their primary concerns and the conflicts they had to face to optimize their spending in addition to the conflicts they would face if they failed to do so. The recipients would understand that a significant shift in value – from struggling with spending to controlling spending – had already started to happen the moment our package came through their door. If they picked up the phone and dialed, their story would move in a positive direction.

Within a few months, our client had secured meetings with CEOs of 13 target banks. Not only had the campaign cost less than Aquanima would have spent on two years of PR, but it offered far more rapid, predictable and manageable results.

We have worked with many companies that think of direct mail as a postcard with an offer – if you send out enough of them, someone is bound to respond. But to make a strong impact, share relevant stories, and bring a specific audience to action, direct marketing – when done well – is a business' best friend. And a good story is direct mail's best friend.

Does it have characters? Does it revolve around life-changing events where significant shifts in values happen? Is there a Big Bad Wolf, a Pillsbury Doughboy, or some opponent that your business had to overcome?

The opponent doesn't have to be a person. Think of it as an opposing force. Perhaps it's something about the social or economic landscape. Perhaps it's a competitor. Perhaps it's an attitude or belief among your customers. It could be a pricing challenge, a delivery challenge…

The drama represents the time or times when expectation and reality didn't meet – when the little pigs, who expected to stay with their mother forever, were sent away to live on their own. When the train of toys heading to the town beyond the mountain broke down.

Is your hero the CEO who brought the company back from the brink of disaster into the best service or product company in its market? Or is it an engineer, a driver, a receptionist or a customer? Perhaps the hero is a product. Sometimes CEOs are simply great administrators, but other parts of the business are heroic in their accomplishments and stories. What's your story, and how do you make it match your purpose in telling it?

CHAPTER 9

TELLING YOUR STORY -
THE LITTLE
WORKBOOK
THAT CAN

The following pages offer you a chance to start your pipeline of stories worthy of publicizing and repeating. While we haven't conducted an official survey, we've met many people in business who read business books like this one. Of those books, many feature exercises or mini workbooks. Yet only a handful of readers actually do the exercises. These are the ones who best remember – and have best implemented – the lessons from the books they read. We encourage you to do the same.

You'll notice that we repeat certain concepts numerous times within these pages. As marketers, we understand the old advertising adage, "reach and frequency." Once we've reached you – and we assume we have if you're reading this – the more we repeat, the more you retain. The following exercises will not only seal this book's lessons in your mind, but will get you started on creating the stories that will change your business forever.

EXERCISE 1: YOUR AUDIENCES

Quickly jot down the most important audiences for your business. With each one, write:

- The audience (be as specific as possible)
- Why you wish to impress this audience
- What this audience cares about most (not in terms of your products, but in terms of life and work. Think about Tom and Julie Adams and what they cared about most).

Repeat this for each of your most important audience segments. Remember, if you lump all your audiences into one segment, you'll end up with a watered-down description that won't help you influence anyone.

EXERCISE 2: ONE STORY EACH

For each audience segment you identified on the previous page, think of one story that your business could share – one story that could touch upon the issues that audience cares about most. Write a few bullets for each, but do not write any sentences. These are simply your notes. For each story, write down:

- Title
- Topic
- How it's relevant to the issues that the specific audience cares about most

EXERCISE 3: DEVELOPING YOUR WINNER

Look at the notes you wrote in the previous pages and think about the audiences that the stories mean to impress. Choose one story. Perhaps it's the one that impresses the most important audience for your business today. Or perhaps you will choose the one where you feel you have the most memorable and compelling story, even though it's for an audience that may not be the most important to you right now.

For that story, write down:
- The story's main characters. These can be inside the company, outside the company, or a combination.
- Gaps between expectation and result. Remember, this can be from a variety of point of views. For Terraclime Geothermal, the gap happened to Tom and Julie Adams, when they expected an idyllic life in Tom's family home but came to a very different result. There may be many such gaps for different characters in your story.
- Most importantly, your story's events. Remember, a story event creates meaningful change in the life situation of a character.

EXERCISE 4: FLESH OUT THE EVENTS

For each event, write down:

- How that event can be expressed as a change in values (review story values in Chapter 3)
- How that event was brought about through conflict – or any conflict that might be associated with that event

EXERCISE 5: BRING IT TOGETHER

On this page, fill each rectangle with the appropriate information. Now you have a picture of your story. How will you tell it: through writing, video, advertisement, direct marketing? Whether you're the one to get this story out or whether you'll ask someone to produce this story for you, such as your marketing manager or a communications agency, this is the page that helps you to keep track of what you will do. Rip it out, photocopy it, and hand it to anyone working on this story with you. Then start from Exercise 1 for the next story!

Audience and key concerns/issues	Characters and why the audience will relate to them
Story events with value shifts and gaps between expectation and result	Ultimate meaningful change and value shift from the story and notable conflicts

CHAPTER 10

OUR TOP 10
RULES OF THE ROAD

Keep the following tips in mind as you work on your stories. You can find many more tips if you look more deeply into storytelling. We're sticking to the critical ones, because we know that too much information won't help. In fact, too much information will only keep you from getting your first stories done and out the door.

1. **Show, don't tell**. Remember the example we used in the first pages of this book: *"I went to work late last night and found my business partner lying on the floor naked with scratch marks all over his body."* That's showing. We never had to explain that he was injured – we never had to "tell." Or: Julie Adams felt sick every time she touched her house's thermostat. You're not sure what's wrong, but you know things aren't looking good for Julie and it has something to do with heating and cooling. Showing helps a human audience visualize what's happening and feel it at the same time. Telling only provides information - we don't connect with it.

2. **It's not all positive, but there's a positive ending**. Depressing stories don't sell products and services. Even nonprofits that work with terribly difficult situations will tell you about success stories to keep you interested. Take this lesson to heart. Nobody wants to work with you when they associate you with bad endings.

3. **Get to the point – it's business, not literature**. We don't need to know that Julie is a soccer mom, and we definitely don't need to see Stu on his motorcycle… unless in some way it relates to the point. Watch one of your favorite movies and notice how every scene advances the story in some way. Even when you love a detail or a passage, if it doesn't further the story, leave it out. In writing, this is called killing your darlings – getting rid of things you adore that won't do anything for anyone else.

4. **Heart matters**. Businesses often shy away from emotion, but remember that your customers are human, even if you are selling to their businesses. Your story characters should experience real emotional ups and downs as we all do.

Reddit's Alexis Ohanian has trouble keeping it together in his video – that draws us in on a primal, emotional level. It's okay to talk to the heart.

5. **No purpose, no story**. If you don't expect the story to create some reaction – be it as intangible as "they will remember me" or as tangible as "they will want to buy from this product," then don't waste your time on it. You have more important things to do.

6. **Show your authority, don't tell it**. Yes, we're repeating a bit of #1. It bears repeating, because the best way to share your competencies is to show them at work. If you're about to say or write, "We're the expert in…" consider how you might show that without ever telling it. Is it that Jim, who spent 16 years teaching mechanical engineering, explained to Tom how the geothermal system would work with his existing ducting? Is it Stu showing his customer how to use the product more effectively in his installation? If you can show it without telling it, your audience will get the message better than when you tell it.

7. **Features and benefits are boring**. Stories should be exciting. If you or anyone else working on the story find it boring, your audience certainly will. Either spice it up, or move on to another story. Think of Apple. Apple won't sell you on how many pixels its latest and greatest screen offers; it'll sell you on how life-like your kids will look on the new screen.

8. **Be honest**. No matter what you sell, you're asking prospects and customers to take a risk. Give them every reason to trust you. It takes much more evidence and time to build trust with people than to destroy it. One mistake, bad review or erroneous/misleading statement can instantly break the trust with prospects and customers.

9. **Choose your characters strategically**. Whose story is your audience more likely to believe – that of an internal product-marketing specialist or a customer? Chances are it's the customer, but not every time. Some companies even

empower unlikely employees to tell their stories, especially through social channels as this creates a genuine voice and unique source of information for those outside the company.

10. **Get it done**. The first story is the hardest. Get one done and make it a model for more. You will not regret it, and you will be thrilled when you hear someone repeating a story you told effectively.

OUR FOUR TOP TRAPS

We've identified many storytelling traps in business. While these top four probably don't apply to you…

- **The "cool-factor" trap**. Have you ever walked out of a movie thinking, "great effects, crappy story?" While your business probably doesn't have Hollywood budgets for storytelling, you can easily fall into the same trap. Using design, video, flashy animations and even simple images, we sometimes forget about telling a good story. Just like that movie with the great effects, the one that you can't quite remember (and by the way, who starred in it?) your story, no matter how dressed up, will be forgotten if it doesn't include… well, a story.

- **The "we're awesome" trap**. Remember Stu's video story and how he was probably thinking, "I think this is great stuff, so my audiences will as well." We use the following statement as a mantra in our agency: We are not the target audience. This keeps us thinking on behalf of the audience and helps us to avoid the assumption that our own values, likes and dislikes apply to everyone else.

- **The "everything but the kitchen sink" trap**. Also called "the never-ending story trap" or "content diarrhea trap." This generally happens when too many chefs are involved in cooking up the story. Joe in engineering wants to put in a bit of the science behind the product, and Roger in product management thinks the story must include a bit of the competitive landscape. Mary in sales wants a description of features and benefits, and the CEO wants to throw in something about a partner company. Yikes! To keep things clear, appoint a story-master and give that person the authority to say no. If Roger's idea doesn't make it, he'll have another chance, perhaps in a story focused only on his perspective. If Roger happens to be the boss, then maybe you have to let someone else's idea drop… or dial in your courage and tell the boss what he doesn't want hear.

- **Worst of all: The "not getting it done" trap**. Many companies have grown on relationships and word of mouth, or enjoyed dominance in a market before competitors cropped up. Not getting it done – not getting great stories into the marketplace – won't stop a great company from growing. But getting those stories out will grow your competitive advantages, increase your reputation's longevity, and ensure you're not leaving money on the table.

The businesses that invest time and resources into telling their stories gain enormous mind-share and market-share as a reward, and great stories often outlast a company's competitive advantages. Help your business generate compelling and memorable stories, and you will never look back.

IN MEMORIAM – DON'T KILL YOUR GOOD STORIES

This book was written by people whose compensation depends on telling good stories for their clients. Cumulatively, we have worked with thousands of businesses over a 150+ years of marketing.

Each of those businesses is run by people, and all of those people have amazing stories.

Some stories focus on unlikely victories, like a small company beating an industry giant. Others address amazing solutions created through hard work and innovation. The stories make us laugh, cry, and revel in the roller coaster of human achievement.

Unfortunately, we've also seen a massive disconnect between the great stories businesses have and the stories they create and put into the world. Stilted language. Watered-down content. Advertisements, white papers, spec sheets and brochures that can put to sleep even the most caffeinated audiences.

We briefly mentioned the notion of "killing your darlings." Most of us understand that it refers to a turn of phrase, scene or image that you love so much you don't want to get rid of it, even though it doesn't really fit in.

Whether or not you're able to kill your darlings, we hope that this book will help you avoid killing your stories. Use the book. Create great stories. Succeed.

NOTES

Rabid Fox – Making Your Business Stories Compelling and Memorable

NOTES

NOTES

ABOUT THE AUTHOR

Nicolas Boillot is CEO of HB Agency, an integrated marketing agency serving customers in business-to-business and business-to-consumer markets. He has led campaigns for brands ranging from HP to Gore Bike Wear, Fairchild Semiconductor to Harvard University. He plays an active role as a Middlebury College alumnus, where he co-founded MiddCORE, an intensive series of courses and programs focused on Creativity, Opportunity, Risk and Entrepreneurship.

Nicolas is an avid writer of fiction and non-fiction, and this is his first business book. He welcomes comments or inquiries, and can be reached through HB Agency.

Nicolas lives in Williamsburg, Massachusetts, with his wife and son.

www.ingramcontent.com/pod-product-compliance
Lightning Source LLC
Chambersburg PA
CBHW060632210326
41520CB00010B/1576